LITTLE LEONARDO'S™

Fascinating World
of the ARTS

Illustrated by
GREG PAPROCKI

Written by
BOB COOPER

GIBBS SMITH
TO ENRICH AND INSPIRE HUMANKIND

The **ARTS** are all about your imagination! Anything you can dream of you can create with some type of art.

ARTISTS use special tools and instruments to create pictures, sculptures, designs, music, and other things, such as DRAWING with pencil and paper . . .

. . . DESIGNING with a COMPUTER . . .

. . . PAINTING with OILS and ACRYLICS . . .

Leonardo da Vinci
1452-1519

Leonardo da Vinci (1452-1519) was born in Italy, the son of a gentleman of Florence. He made significant contributions to many different disciplines, including anatomy, botany, geology, astronomy, architecture, paleontology, and cartography.

He is one of the greatest and most influential painters of all time, creating masterpieces such as the *Mona Lisa* and *The Last Supper*. And his imagination led him to create designs for things such as an armored car, scuba gear, a parachute, a revolving bridge, and flying machines. Many of these ideas were so far ahead of their time that they weren't built until centuries later.

He is the original "Renaissance Man" whose genius extended to all five areas of today's STEAM curriculum: Science, Technology, Engineering, the Arts, and Mathematics.

You can find more information on Leonardo da Vinci in *Who Was Leonardo da Vinci?* by Roberta Edwards (Grosset & Dunlap, 2005), *Magic Tree House Fact Tracker: Leonardo da Vinci* by Mary Pope Osborne and Natalie Pope Bryce (Random House, 2009), and *Leonardo da Vinci for Kids: His Life and Ideas* by Janis Herbert (Chicago Review Press, 1998).

... SCULPTING with clay ...

... taking PHOTOGRAPHS with a CAMERA ...

... DANCING in a BALLET ...
and anything else you can imagine.

Humans have been creating
art for thousands of years.

Some of the oldest art decorated the
walls of our prehistoric ancestors' caves.

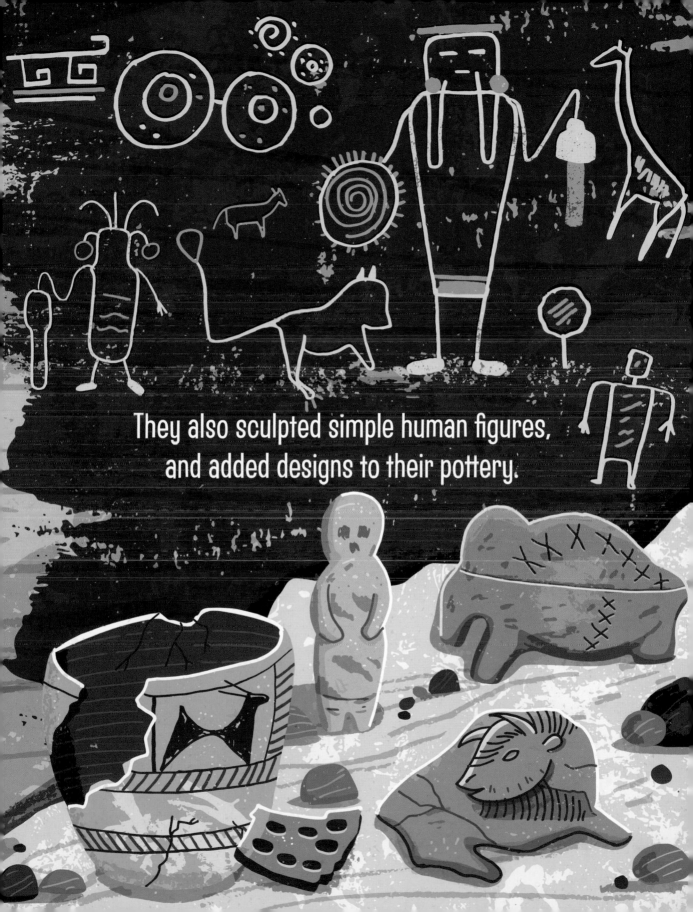

They also sculpted simple human figures,
and added designs to their pottery.

Art is everywhere. From when you wake up in the morning until you go to sleep at night, art is a part of everything you do.

One of the most basic forms of VISUAL ART is DRAWING. . .

. . . where a PEN, PENCIL, CRAYON, or other tool is used to add LINES, SHAPES, and COLORS to a drawing surface like a piece of PAPER.

PAINTERS create shapes and colors by using **PAINTBRUSHES** and **PALETTE KNIVES** to apply layers of **PAINT** to a surface like **CANVAS**.

SCULPTORS can create even more realistic art in three dimensions from a solid piece of **CLAY**, or a rock like **MARBLE**.

Different forms of visual art are used to DESIGN things so that they look more appealing to people who buy them and use them.

GRAPHIC DESIGNERS create all kinds of COMMERCIAL ART, like soft drink cans, company logos, book covers, websites, movie credits, and magazine ads.

WRITERS, POETS, SONGWRITERS, and MUSICIANS use their imaginations to create compositions of words and music.

Instead of pencils or paintbrushes, LANGUAGE
is the tool they use to write SONGS,
POEMS, STORIES, and NOVELS, creating unforgettable
people, places, and events.

MUSIC can instantly change your mood. It can make you feel good or bad, happy or sad, excited or mad.

Different MUSICAL INSTRUMENTS, like pianos, drums, guitars, trumpets, and violins, make different kinds of sounds, and can work together to make beautiful music.

SINGING adds another important piece to the music.

Many different kinds of artists, using their skills with language, music, visual arts, and design, all work together with ACTORS to create DRAMATIC entertainment like MOVIES, PLAYS, CARTOONS, and VIDEO GAMES.

ARCHITECTS and INDUSTRIAL DESIGNERS

use science and mathematics along with art and design to create houses, cars, and other complex buildings and machines that are functional *and* look beautiful.

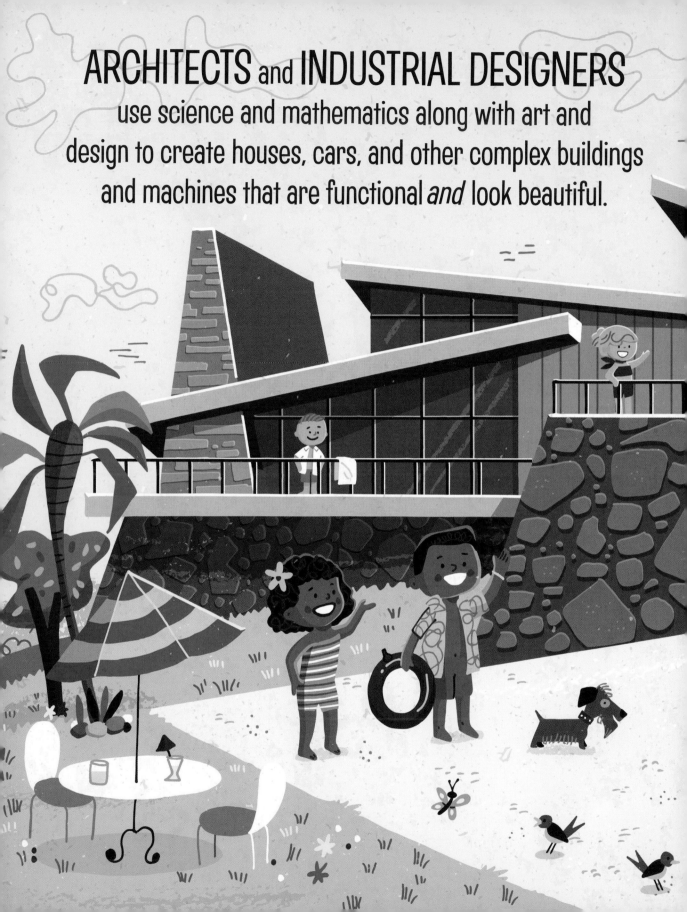

Computers now perform many of the tasks that artists, designers, and musicians used to do with their special tools and instruments.

A computer can sound like a piano, paint like a paintbrush, and take a photo like a camera—which makes it easier for anyone to create their own artistic masterpiece!

Artists create things from their imaginations.

What kinds of things can *you* imagine?

What kind of artist would *you* like to be?

GLOSSARY

ACRYLIC (uh-KRILL-uck): A type of paint that dries much faster than oil paint.

ACTOR: A person who plays a character in a movie, play, or TV show.

ARCHITECT (ARE-kuh-tect): Someone who designs buildings.

ARTIST: A person who creates works of art, such as painters and sculptors.

ARTS: A group of creative skills where imagination is used to produce works of art that often express ideas or feelings.

BALLET (bal-LAY): A type of dancing performed on stage using music, dance, and costumes to tell a story.

CAMERA (KAM-ruh): A device used for taking photographs.

CANVAS (CAN-vuss): A specially prepared piece of cloth used by an artist to paint on.

CARTOON: An animated movie or TV show.

CLAY: A sticky material found in the earth that can be sculpted into different shapes. It becomes hard when baked or dried.

COLOR: A visual quality such as red, green, white, or black, created by the way an object reflects light.

COMMERCIAL ART (come-MER-shull art): Art that's used to help sell a product or idea.

COMPUTER (come-PEW-turr): An electronic machine that stores and works with large amounts of information. It can play music, movies, and games, and help create many types of art.

CRAYON (KRAY-on): A stick of wax used for drawing. It can come in many different colors.

DANCING: A series of movements usually performed in time to music.

DESIGN (duh-ZINE): Using different types of art to create more complex things like commercial products; or to create plans and drawings that show how something is made.

DRAMA (DRAW-muh): Entertainment like movies and plays that tell stories about people and life through action and words.

DRAWING: Creating a picture with lines, shapes, and colors using pencils, pens, crayons, or other drawing tools.

GRAPHIC DESIGNER (GRAF-ick duh-ZINE-urr): Someone who creates designs, often combining words and pictures, that are used to help sell things.

INDUSTRIAL DESIGNER (in-DUST-ree-uhl duh-ZINE-urr): Someone who designs products made by machines, like cars, furniture, and vacuum cleaners.

LANGUAGE (LANG-gwudge): A system of words that people use to describe the world around them and to express their thoughts and feelings.

LINE: A long, narrow mark made by a drawing tool that often shows the outline of an object.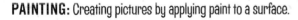

MARBLE (MAR-bull): A type of hard stone that is used to create sculptures.

MOVIE: A recorded series of images that combined in a sequence tells a dramatic story.

MUSIC: A series of sounds that are sung or played on musical instruments. Someone who plays music is called a MUSICIAN.

MUSICAL INSTRUMENT (MEW-zih-cull IN-struh-munt): A device such as a violin, piano, or flute used to make music.

NOVEL: A long story about imaginary characters and events.

OIL: A type of paint that takes longer to dry than acrylic but keeps its color better.

PAINT: A liquid that creates a thin colored layer after being spread on a surface with a tool like a paintbrush. An artist that works with paint is called a PAINTER.

PAINTBRUSH: A brush used for spreading paint on a surface.

PAINTING: Creating pictures by applying paint to a surface.

PALETTE KNIFE (PAL-lut nyf): A flexible knife used by painters to mix colors and apply paint to a surface.

PAPER: Thin sheets of material used for writing, drawing, or printing.

PEN: A writing tool that uses ink.

PENCIL: A tool for writing and drawing, usually made of a thin solid strip of graphite, colored wax, or charcoal inside a wooden casing.

PHOTOGRAPH (FOE-tuh-graf): A picture made by a camera.

PIGMENT (PIG-munt): The thing in liquids like paint and ink that gives them their color.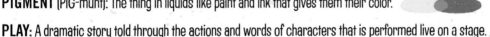

PLAY: A dramatic story told through the actions and words of characters that is performed live on a stage.

POEM (PO-um): A type of very expressive writing, with lines that often rhyme. Someone who writes poems is known as a POET.

SCULPTING (SKULP-ting): Making a piece of three-dimensional art by carving or molding materials like clay or marble. An artist who sculpts is called a SCULPTOR.

SHAPE: The form or outline of an object.

SINGING: Using your voice to make musical sounds in the form of a song.

SONGWRITER (SONG-rye-tur): Someone who writes the words or music for a SONG.

STORY: A description of imaginary people and events told as a form of entertainment.

VIDEO GAME: An electronic game where players control the actions of characters and images on a TV or computer screen.

VISUAL ART (VIJ-you-ull art): A type of art such as drawing, painting, and sculpture that can be appreciated just by looking at it.

WRITER: Someone who creates stories and novels.

Manufactured in Hong Kong in January 2018 by Toppan Printing

First Edition
22 21 20 19 18   5 4 3 2 1

Published by
Gibbs Smith
P.O. Box 667
Layton, Utah 84041

1.800.835.4993 orders
www.gibbs-smith.com

Designed by Greg Paprocki

Gibbs Smith books are printed on either recycled, 100% post-consumer waste, FSC-certified papers or on paper produced from sustainable PEFC-certified forest/controlled wood source. Learn more at www.pefc.org.

Library of Congress Control Number: 2017947919
ISBN: 978-1-4236-4873-4

Some famous people in the arts . . .

Michelangelo Buonarroti (1475–1564)
Like his contemporary Leonardo da Vinci, Michelangelo was considered a Renaissance man who excelled in many different art forms, including painting and sculpting. Best known for his painting of the Sistine Chapel ceiling and the sculpture of David, he was considered the greatest living artist during his lifetime. He also made important contributions to architecture.

William Shakespeare (1564–1616)
He's recognized as the greatest writer in the English language and the greatest playwright of all time. His thirty-eight plays have been translated into every major language, and are still performed more than any other playwright's. They include some of the most popular and well-known works of literature in the world, such as *Hamlet, Romeo and Juliet, A Midsummer Night's Dream,* and *Macbeth.*

Jane Austen (1775–1817)
She was known largely for the six novels she wrote, including *Pride and Prejudice* and *Sense and Sensibility.* Though not well known during her lifetime, her work gained in reputation after her death. Her novels have remained some of the most popular in the English language and have inspired many movies.

Frank Lloyd Wright (1867–1959)

He was an incredibly influential architect and designer who designed more than a thousand buildings over a career of more than seventy years. It was especially important to him to design buildings that were in harmony with both people and the environment, best shown in his design for the Fallingwater house. Wright was formally recognized as the greatest American architect of all time in 1991.

Dorothea Lange (1895–1965)
A pioneering photographer best known for her stark photos of the Great Depression. Through her photos, she was able to humanize many of the people hit hardest by the Depression. In 1940 she became the first woman awarded a Guggenheim Fellowship. She was a major influence on the development of documentary photography.

Frida Kahlo (1907–1954)
Considered one of Mexico's greatest artists, she mostly painted self-portraits in a folk art style that combined realism with fantasy. Her work especially celebrates Mexican traditions and female creativity. She was the first Mexican artist to be featured at the famous Louvre in Paris.

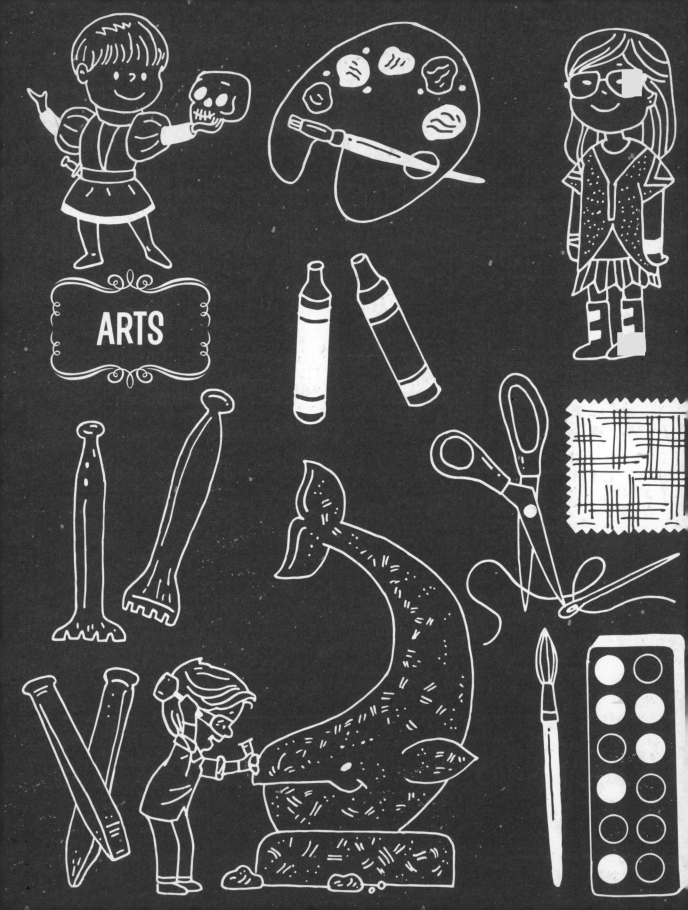

ARTS